# My Sight Word List



| | | |
|---|---|---|
| a | in | said |
| and | is | see |
| away | it | the |
| big | jump | three |
| blue | little | to |
| can | look | two |
| come | make | up |
| down | me | we |
| find | my | where |
| for | not | yellow |
| funny | one | you |
| go | day | |
| help | play | |
| here | red | |
| I | run | |

Name: ______________________ Date: ______________________

Today is: Monday | Tuesday | Wednesday | Thursday | Friday

Direction: Trace and read the sentences.

| **amusement** | **pistolet** | **courir** | **soleil** |
|---|---|---|---|
|  | 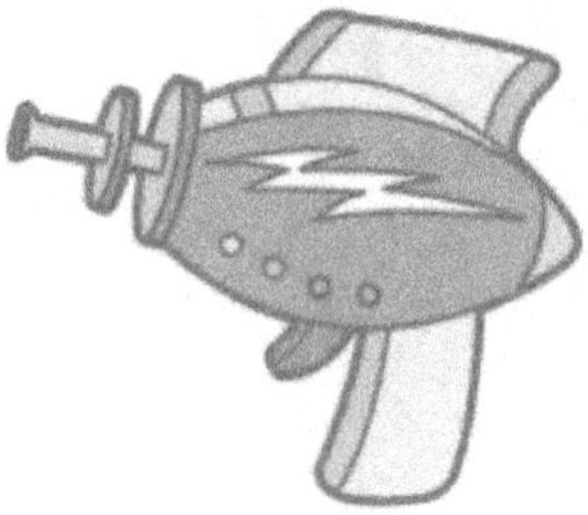 |  |  |
| geniet | geweer | run | son |

They are having fun.

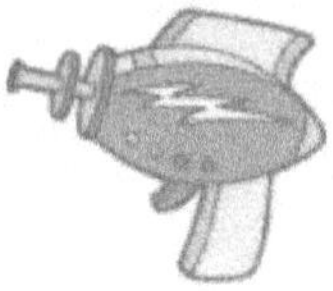

He has a gun.

The bear is running.

The sun is smiling.

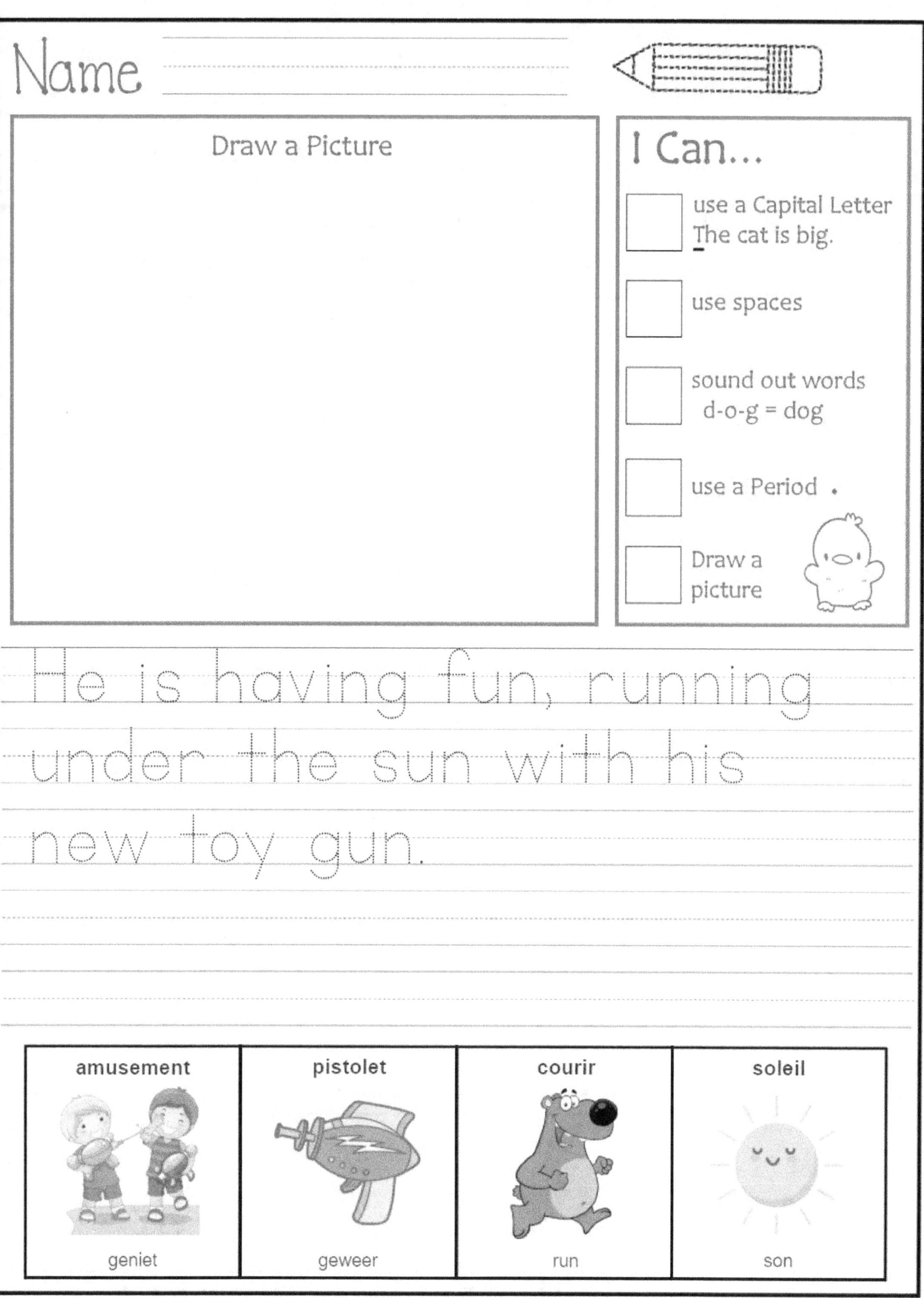

Name

Draw a Picture

I Can...

use a Capital Letter
The cat is big.

use spaces

sound out words
d-o-g = dog

use a Period .

Draw a picture

He is having fun, running under the sun with his new toy gun.

amusement
geniet

pistolet
geweer

courir
run

soleil
son

Name: ___________________ Date: ___________

Today is: Monday  Tuesday  Wednesday

Thursday  Friday

Direction: Trace and read the sentences.

| sac | chiffon | étiquette | remuer |
|---|---|---|---|
| sak | lap | tag | swaaiende |

He has many bags.

I see a rag.

I see a tag.

Its tail is wagging.

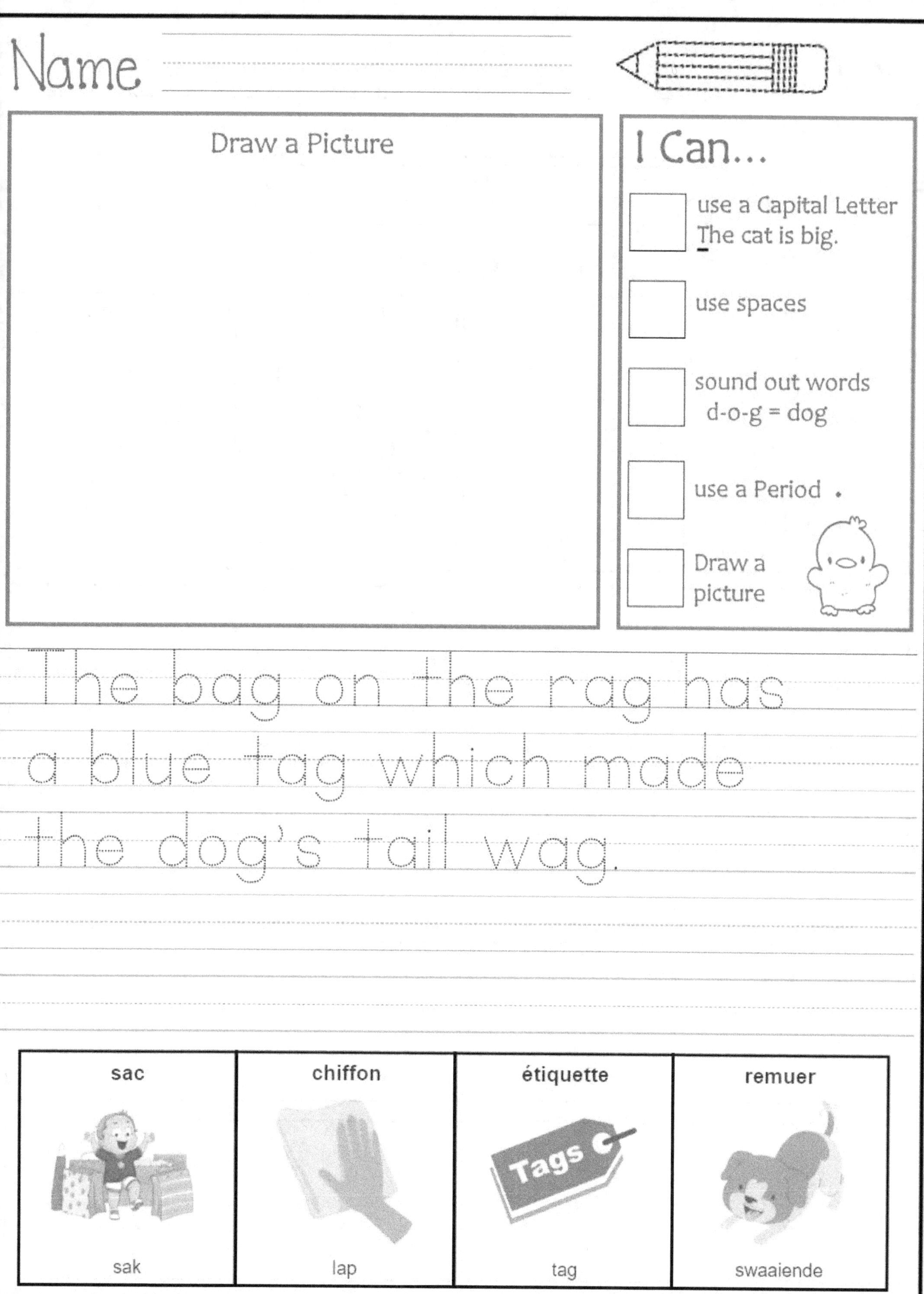

Name

## Draw a Picture

## I Can...

- ☐ use a Capital Letter
  <u>T</u>he cat is big.
- ☐ use spaces
- ☐ sound out words
  d-o-g = dog
- ☐ use a Period .
- ☐ Draw a picture

The bag on the rag has
a blue tag which made
the dog's tail wag.

| sac | chiffon | étiquette | remuer |
|-----|---------|-----------|--------|
| sak | lap | tag | swaaiende |

Name: ______________________ Date: ______________________

Today is: Monday Tuesday Wednesday Thursday Friday

Direction: Trace and read the sentences.

| canettes | homme | la poêle | van |
|---|---|---|---|
|  |  |  |  |
| blikkies | man | pan | van |

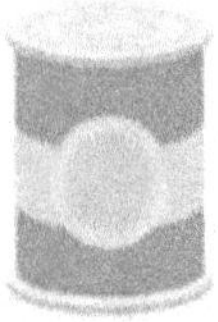

I see a can of soda.

The man is happy.

The pan is dirty.

I see a big van.

Draw a Picture

## I Can...

- [ ] use a Capital Letter
  The cat is big.

- [ ] use spaces

- [ ] sound out words
  d-o-g = dog

- [ ] use a Period .

- [ ] Draw a picture

The man who was driving a van ran over a can and a pan.

| canettes | homme | la poêle | van |
|---|---|---|---|
| blikkies | man | pan | van |

Name: _______________  Date: _______________

Today is: [ Monday ] [ Tuesday ] [ Wednesday ]
[ Thursday ] [ Friday ]

Direction: Trace and read the sentences.

| couper | intestin | cabane | écrou |
|--------|----------|--------|-------|
| sny | gut | hut | neut |

He cut his nails.

He has a gut.

This is a small hut.

It is holding a nut.

A boy swallowed a nut and it got stuck in his belly. He had to get his gut cut open in the hut.

| couper | intestin | cabane | écrou |
|---|---|---|---|
| sny | gut | hut | neut |

Name: ________________  Date: __________

Today is: [ Monday ] [ Tuesday ] [ Wednesday ]
[ Thursday ] [ Friday ]

Direction: Trace and read the sentences.

| graisse | chat | chapeau | tapis |
|---|---|---|---|
| vet | kat | hoed | mat |

I see a fat dog.

This is my little cat.

I like this hat.

I see a big mat.

The fat cat laid on the mat that was a hat pattern.

Name: ____________________ Date: ____________________

Today is: Monday | Tuesday | Wednesday | Thursday | Friday

Direction: Trace and read the sentences.

| taxi | laboratoire | languette | crabe |
| --- | --- | --- | --- |
|  |  |  |  |
| taxi | laboratorium | blad | krap |

The cab is fast.

The lab is exciting.

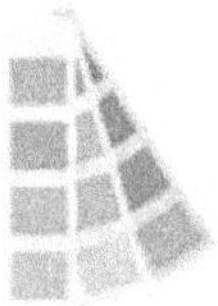

The tab is long.

We found a crab.

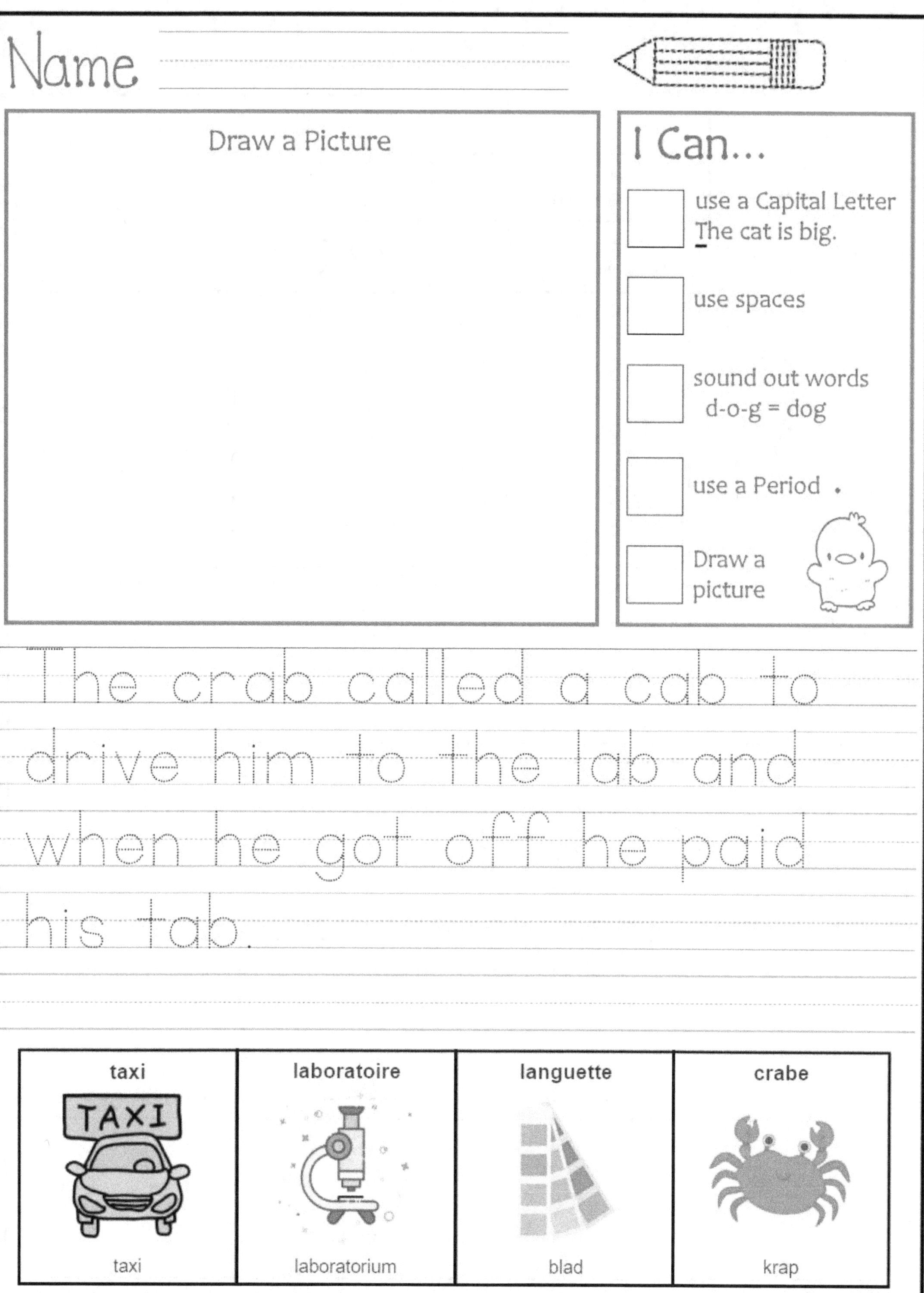

Name

Draw a Picture

I Can...

use a Capital Letter
The cat is big.

use spaces

sound out words
d-o-g = dog

use a Period .

Draw a
picture

The crab called a cab to
drive him to the lab and
when he got off he paid
his tab.

taxi
taxi

laboratoire
laboratorium

languette
blad

crabe
krap

Name: ____________________ Date: ____________________

Today is: Monday Tuesday Wednesday Thursday Friday

Direction: Trace and read the sentences.

| jambon | confiture | mouton | palourde |
| --- | --- | --- | --- |
|  |  |  |  |
| ham | konfyt | skape | clam |

I like to eat ham.

We like to eat jam.

The ram is big.

The clam is pretty.

## Draw a Picture

## I Can...

- [ ] use a Capital Letter
  The cat is big.
- [ ] use spaces
- [ ] sound out words
  d-o-g = dog
- [ ] use a Period .
- [ ] Draw a picture

The clam gave the ram ham. Then the ram gave the clam jam.

| jambon | confiture | mouton | palourde |
|---|---|---|---|
| ham | konfyt | skape | clam |

Name: _______________ Date: _______________

Today is: Monday  Tuesday  Wednesday  Thursday  Friday

Direction: Trace and read the sentences.

| lit | de premier plan | rouge | mariage |
|---|---|---|---|
| bed | voorste | rooi | troue |

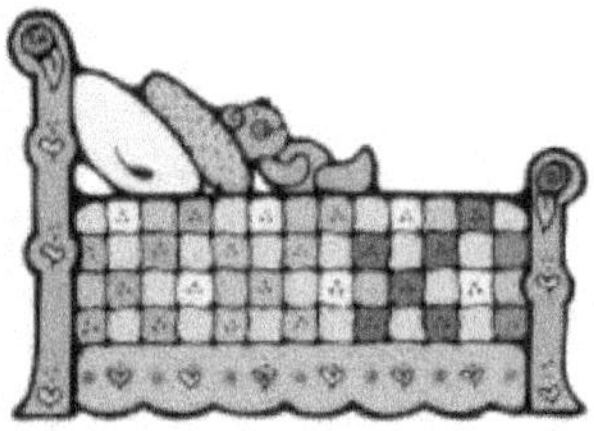

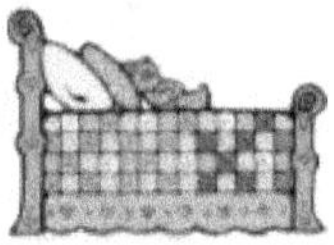

This is my little bed.

He led us to safety.

The apple is red.

He asks her to wed.

# Name

Draw a Picture

## I Can...

- [ ] use a Capital Letter
  The cat is big.
- [ ] use spaces
- [ ] sound out words
  d-o-g = dog
- [ ] use a Period .
- [ ] Draw a picture

When the prince got out of bed, he was led on a red carpet to be wed with the princess.

| lit | de premier plan | rouge | mariage |
|---|---|---|---|
| bed | voorste | rooi | troue |

Name: ____________________ Date: ____________________

Today is: Monday | Tuesday | Wednesday | Thursday | Friday

Direction: Trace and read the sentences.

| mauvais | papa | furieux | triste |
| --- | --- | --- | --- |
|  |  |  |  |
| slegte | pa | mal | hartseer |

This apple is bad.

My dad is very kind.

The reindeer is mad.

The little cat is sad.

## Draw a Picture

## I Can...

- [ ] use a Capital Letter
  The cat is big.
- [ ] use spaces
- [ ] sound out words
  d-o-g = dog
- [ ] use a Period .
- [ ] Draw a picture

I was bad so my dad got mad and now I am so sad.

| mauvais | papa | furieux | triste |
|---|---|---|---|
| slegte | pa | mal | hartseer |

Name: _______________  Date: _______________

Today is: [ Monday ] [ Tuesday ] [ Wednesday ]
[ Thursday ] [ Friday ]

Direction: Trace and read the sentences.

| animal den | poule | écuries | dix |
| --- | --- | --- | --- |
| den | hen | stalle | tien |

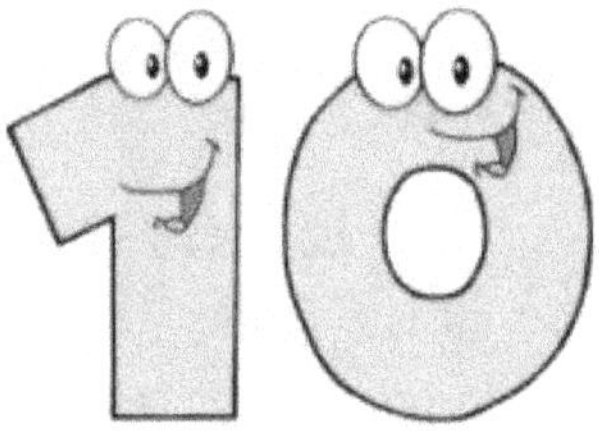

It is a den.

The hens lay eggs.

She has a good pen.

The ten is smiling.

# Name

## Draw a Picture

## I Can...

- [ ] use a Capital Letter
  The cat is big.
- [ ] use spaces
- [ ] sound out words
  d-o-g = dog
- [ ] use a Period .
- [ ] Draw a picture

The hen that lived in the pen laid ten eggs in her den.

| animal den | poule | écuries | dix |
|---|---|---|---|
| den | hen | stalle | tien |

Name: _______________________  Date: _____________

Today is: [ Monday ] [ Tuesday ] [ Wednesday ]
[ Thursday ] [ Friday ]

Direction: Trace and read the sentences.

| gommeux | maman | somme | tambour |
|---|---|---|---|
| gummy | mamma | som | drom |

I like to chew gum.

My mum is kind!

I can do a sum!

The drum is big.

Draw a Picture

## I Can...

- [ ] use a Capital Letter
The cat is big.

- [ ] use spaces

- [ ] sound out words
d-o-g = dog

- [ ] use a Period .

- [ ] Draw a picture

Mum was chewing gum while figuring out the sum of the drum's price.

| gommeux | maman | somme | tambour |
| --- | --- | --- | --- |
| gummy | mamma | som | drom |

Name: ____________________ Date: ____________________

Today is: Monday Tuesday Wednesday Thursday Friday

Direction: Trace and read the sentences.

| offre | cacher | enfant | couvercle |
| --- | --- | --- | --- |
|  |  |  | 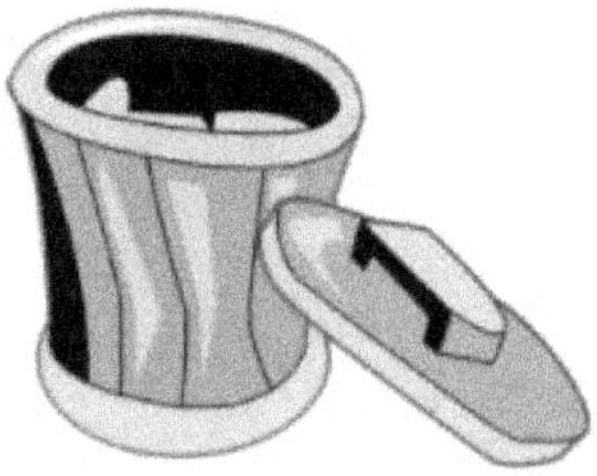 |
| bod | verberg | kind | deksel |

He likes to bid.

He is hiding.

The kid like to play.

I see a lid.

Name ___________

### Draw a Picture

## I Can...

- [ ] use a Capital Letter
  The cat is big.

- [ ] use spaces

- [ ] sound out words
  d-o-g = dog

- [ ] use a Period .

- [ ] Draw a picture

The kid bid a lid for one hundred dollars then hid from his mad parents.

| offre | cacher | enfant | couvercle |
|---|---|---|---|
| bod | verberg | kind | deksel |

Name: _______________ Date: _______________

Today is: [Monday] [Tuesday] [Wednesday]
[Thursday] [Friday]

Direction: Trace and read the sentences.

| **gros** | **creuser** | **porc** | **perruque** |
|---|---|---|---|
| groot | grawe | vark | wig |

That is a big pencil.

He will dig up a hole.

The pig is fat.

She puts on a wig.

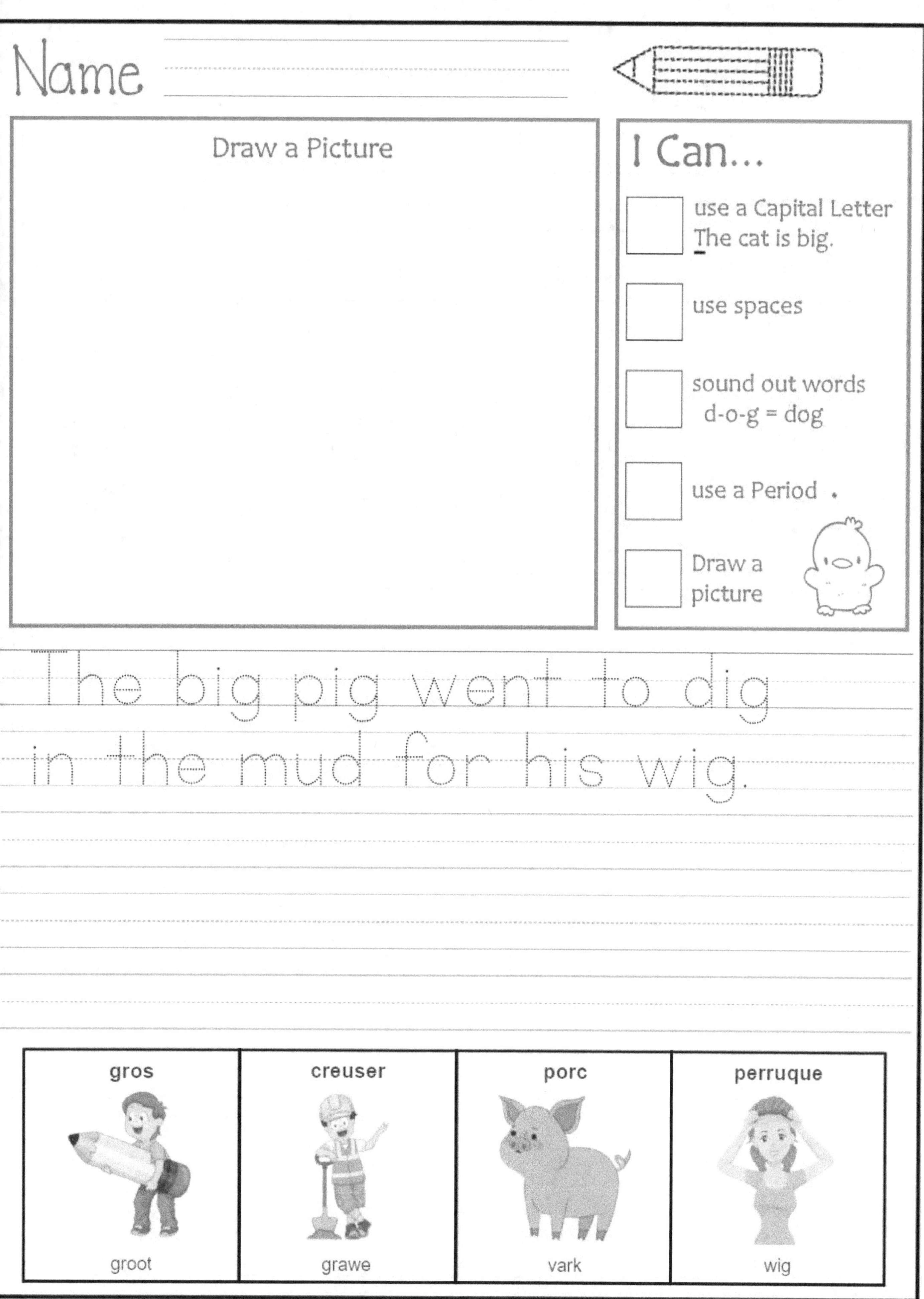

Name
Draw a Picture
I Can...
use a Capital Letter
The cat is big.
use spaces
sound out words
d-o-g = dog
use a Period .
Draw a picture
The big pig went to dig in the mud for his wig.
gros
groot
creuser
grawe
porc
vark
perruque
wig

Name: ____________________ Date: ____________________

Today is: Monday Tuesday Wednesday Thursday Friday

Direction: Trace and read the sentences.

| poubelle | ailette | épingle | gagner |
|---|---|---|---|
|  | 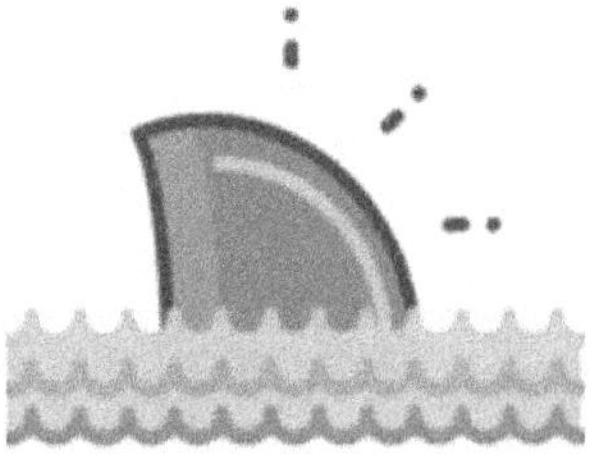 |  |  |
| bin | vin | speld | wen |

It is a recycle bin.

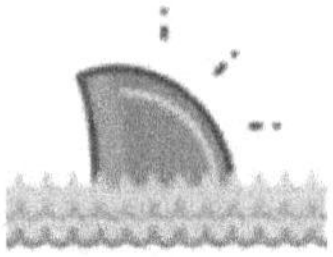

The shark has a fin.

The pin is pointy.

He won the match.

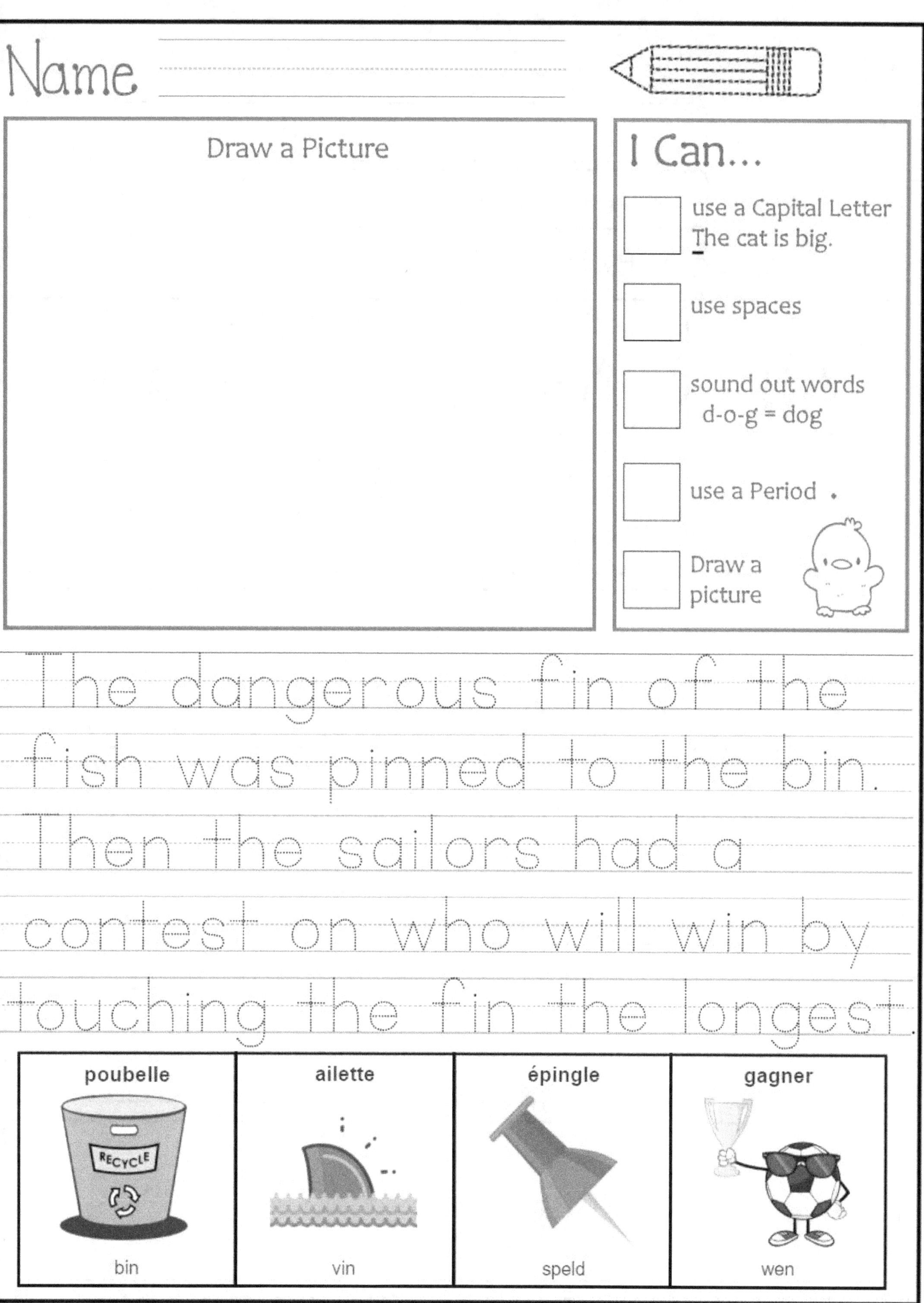


Name

Draw a Picture

I Can...

use a Capital Letter
The cat is big.

use spaces

sound out words
d-o-g = dog

use a Period .

Draw a
picture

The dangerous fin of the
fish was pinned to the bin.
Then the sailors had a
contest on who will win by
touching the fin the longest.

poubelle
ailette
épingle
gagner

RECYCLE

bin
vin
speld
wen

Name: ______________________ Date: ______________________

Today is: Monday Tuesday Wednesday Thursday Friday

Direction: Trace and read the sentences.

| hanche | lèvres | pincer | boisson |
| --- | --- | --- | --- |
|  |  |  |  |
| hip | lippe | nip | drink |

This is my hip.

Her lips are red.

It is nipping its toy.

She is sipping.

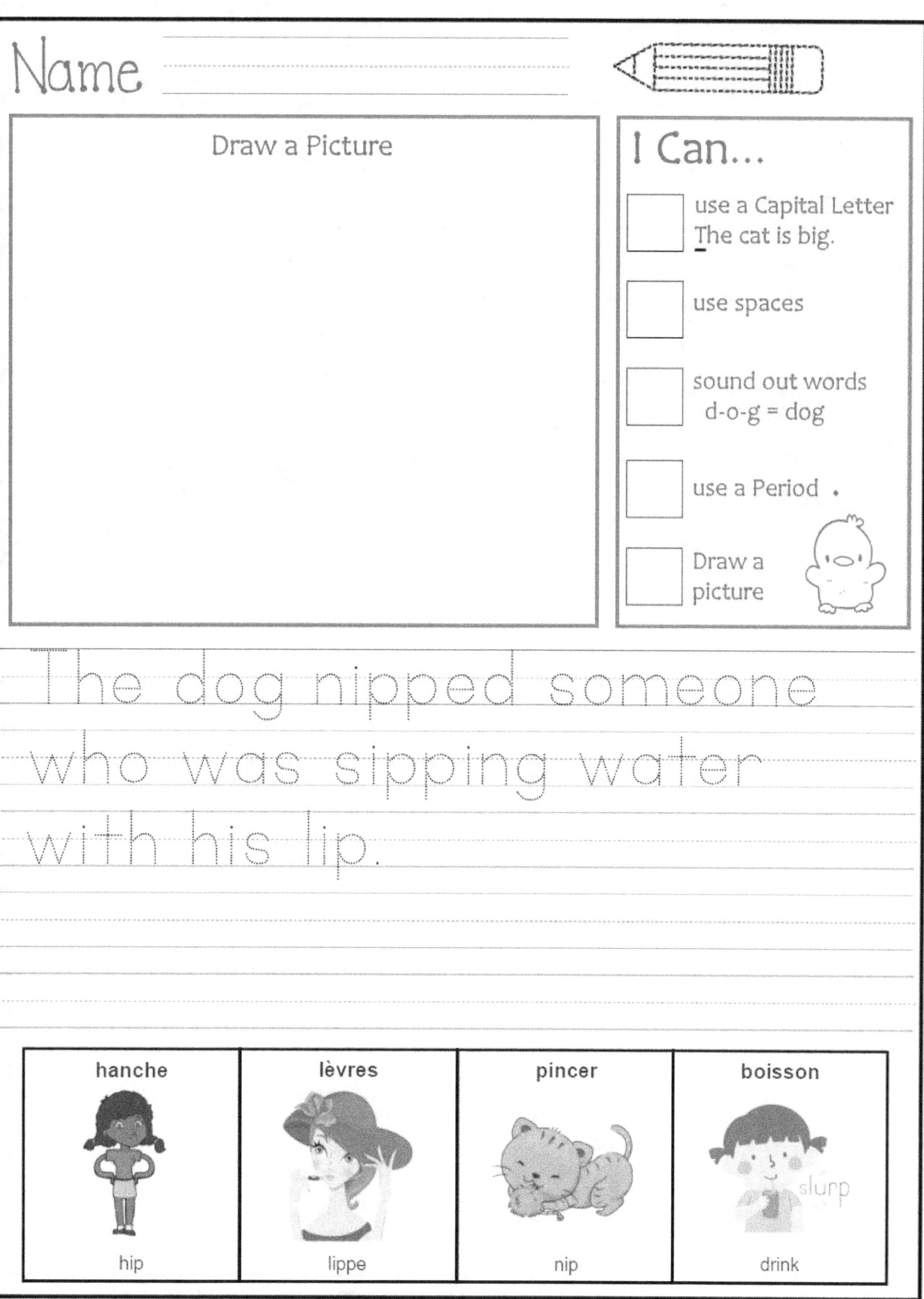


Name

Draw a Picture

I Can...

use a Capital Letter
The cat is big.

use spaces

sound out words
d-o-g = dog

use a Period .

Draw a
picture

The dog nipped someone
who was sipping water
with his lip.

hanche
hip

lèvres
lippe

pincer
nip

boisson
slurp
drink

Name: ______________________ Date: ______________________

Today is: Monday | Tuesday | Wednesday | Thursday | Friday

Direction: Trace and read the sentences.

| en forme | frappé | trousse | asseoir |
| --- | --- | --- | --- |
|  |  | 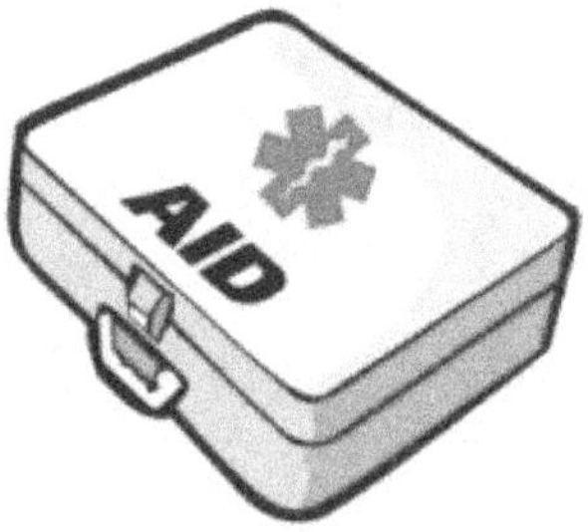<br> |  |
| fiks | getref | kit | sit |

It is perfectly fit.

They hit each other.

That is a safety kit.

He is sitting.

The fit doctor sat then was hit by a kit.

| en forme | frappé | trousse | asseoir |
|---|---|---|---|
| fiks | getref | kit | sit |

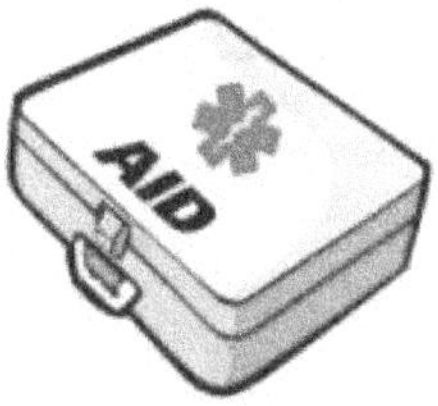

Name: ___________________ Date: ___________

Today is: [Monday] [Tuesday] [Wednesday] [Thursday] [Friday]

Direction: Trace and read the sentences.

| blé | emploi | rob | pleurer |
|---|---|---|---|
| koring | werk | beroof | geroep |

I ate corn on the cob

This is my job.

He is robbing.

The girl is sobbing.

Name

Draw a Picture

I Can...

- [ ] use a Capital Letter The cat is big.
- [ ] use spaces
- [ ] sound out words d-o-g = dog
- [ ] use a Period .
- [ ] Draw a picture

The chef robbed a corn cob and then was sobbing because he had lost his job.

| blé | emploi | rob | pleurer |
|---|---|---|---|
|  |  |  |  |
| koring | werk | beroof | geroep |

Name: _______________ Date: _______________

Today is: Monday  Tuesday  Wednesday  Thursday  Friday

Direction: Trace and read the sentences.

| chien | porc | le jogging | bois |
|---|---|---|---|
| hond | hog | draf | hout |

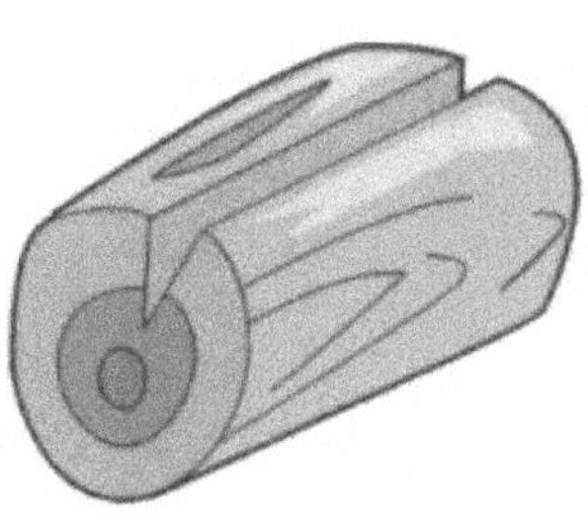

The dog is thrilled.

The hog is big.

She is jogging.

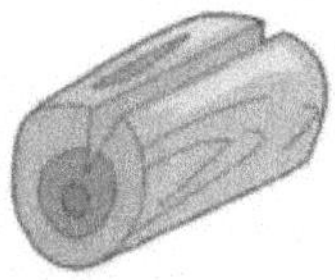

The log is small.

Draw a Picture

## I Can...

- [ ] use a Capital Letter
  The cat is big.
- [ ] use spaces
- [ ] sound out words
  d-o-g = dog
- [ ] use a Period .
- [ ] Draw a picture

The dog and the hog went for a jog but then tripped on a log.

| chien | porc | le jogging | bois |
|---|---|---|---|
| hond | hog | draf | hout |

Name: ________________    Date: ________

Today is: [ Monday ] [ Tuesday ] [ Wednesday ]
[ Thursday ] [ Friday ]

Direction: Trace and read the sentences.

| punaise | étreinte | cruche | agresser |
|---|---|---|---|
| fout | drukkie | beker | beker |

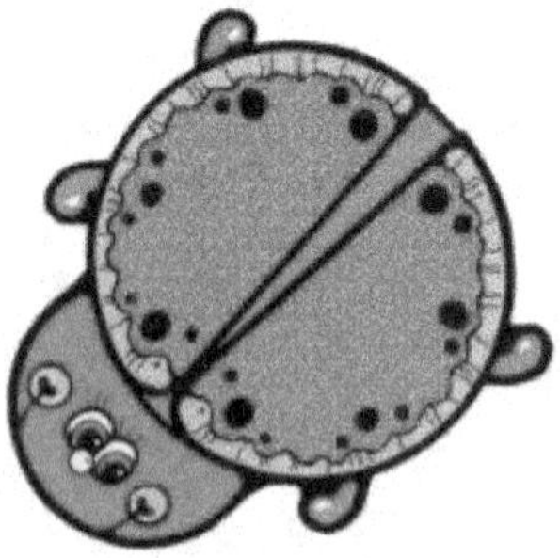

The bug is colorful.

She is hugging.

The jug has milk in it.

He has a mug.

## Draw a Picture

## I Can...

- use a Capital Letter
  The cat is big.
- use spaces
- sound out words
  d-o-g = dog
- use a Period .
- Draw a picture

The bug hugged the jug
and the mug which was
full of jam.

| punaise | étreinte | cruche | agresser |
|---|---|---|---|
| fout | drukkie | beker | beker |

Name: ____________________ Date: ____________________

Today is: Monday Tuesday Wednesday Thursday Friday

Direction: Trace and read the sentences.

| lit | point | chaud | pot |
|---|---|---|---|
|  |  |  |  |
| bed | dot | warm | pot |

This is my cot.

There are many dots.

It is very hot.

He has a plant pot.

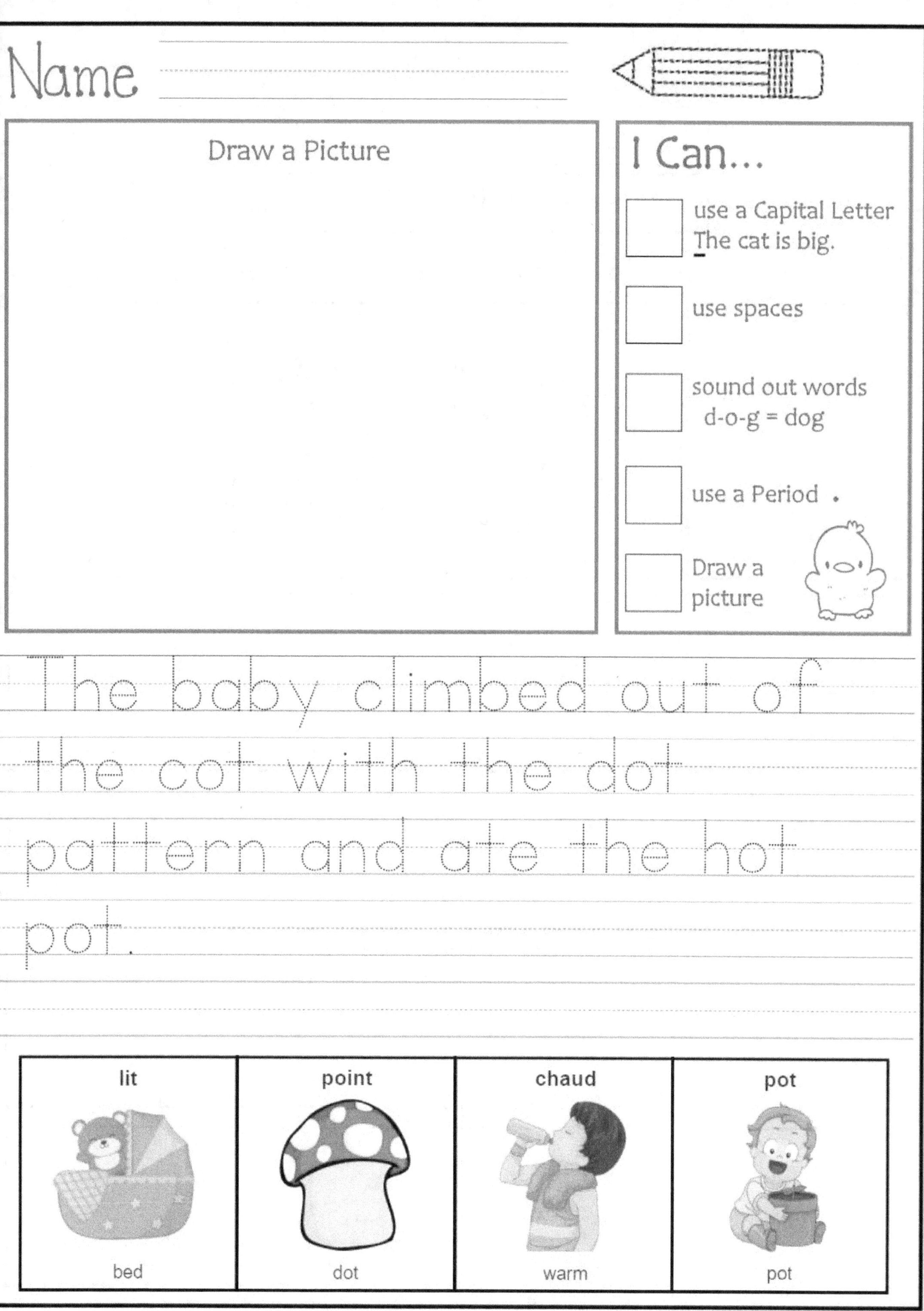

Name

Draw a Picture

I Can...

use a Capital Letter
The cat is big.

use spaces

sound out words
d-o-g = dog

use a Period .

Draw a
picture

The baby climbed out of
the cot with the dot
pattern and ate the hot
pot.

lit
bed

point
dot

chaud
warm

pot
pot

Name: _________________ Date: _________

Today is: [ Monday ] [ Tuesday ] [ Wednesday ]
[ Thursday ] [ Friday ]

Direction: Read the words and make a sentence.

| amusement | pistolet | courir | soleil |
|---|---|---|---|
| geniet | geweer | run | son |

Name

Draw a Picture

I Can...

use a Capital Letter
The cat is big.

use spaces

sound out words
d-o-g = dog

use a Period .

Draw a
picture

Name: _______________    Date: _______________

Today is: [Monday] [Tuesday] [Wednesday]
[Thursday] [Friday]

Name: _________________________ Date: _______________

Today is:  Monday   Tuesday   Wednesday

Thursday   Friday

Direction: Read the words and make a sentence.

| sac | chiffon | étiquette | remuer |
|---|---|---|---|
| sak | lap | tag | swaaiende |

# Name

Draw a Picture

## I Can...

- ☐ use a Capital Letter
  The cat is big.

- ☐ use spaces

- ☐ sound out words
  d-o-g = dog

- ☐ use a Period .

- ☐ Draw a picture

Name: _____________________  Date: _____________________

Today is: Monday  Tuesday  Wednesday  Thursday  Friday

Name: _______________  Date: _______________

Today is: Monday | Tuesday | Wednesday | Thursday | Friday

Direction: Read the words and make a sentence.

| canettes | homme | la poêle | van |
|---|---|---|---|
| blikkies | man | pan | van |

Name

Draw a Picture

## I Can...

- [ ] use a Capital Letter
  <u>T</u>he cat is big.

- [ ] use spaces

- [ ] sound out words
  d-o-g = dog

- [ ] use a Period .

- [ ] Draw a picture

Name: _______________________  Date: _______________________

Today is: Monday  Tuesday  Wednesday  Thursday  Friday

Name: ______________________  Date: ______________

Today is: | Monday | Tuesday | Wednesday |
| Thursday | Friday |

Direction: Read the words and make a sentence.

| **couper** | **intestin** | **cabane** | **écrou** |
| sny | gut | hut | neut |

___________________________________________

___________________________________________

___________________________________________

___________________________________________

___________________________________________

Name

Draw a Picture

## I Can...

- [ ] use a Capital Letter
  The cat is big.

- [ ] use spaces

- [ ] sound out words
  d-o-g = dog

- [ ] use a Period .

- [ ] Draw a picture

Name: _______________________ Date: _______________

Today is: Monday Tuesday Wednesday Thursday Friday

Name: _______________ Date: _______________

Today is: Monday  Tuesday  Wednesday  Thursday  Friday

Direction: Read the words and make a sentence.

| graisse | chat | chapeau | tapis |
|---|---|---|---|
| vet | kat | hoed | mat |

Name

Draw a Picture

## I Can...

- [ ] use a Capital Letter
  The cat is big.

- [ ] use spaces

- [ ] sound out words
  d-o-g = dog

- [ ] use a Period .

- [ ] Draw a picture

Name: _______________ Date: _______________

Today is: Monday Tuesday Wednesday Thursday Friday

Name: _______________________  Date: _______________

Today is: [Monday] [Tuesday] [Wednesday]
[Thursday] [Friday]

Direction: Read the words and make a sentence.

| taxi | laboratoire | languette | crabe |
|------|-------------|-----------|-------|
| taxi | laboratorium | blad | krap |

Name

Draw a Picture

## I Can...

- [ ] use a Capital Letter
  The cat is big.

- [ ] use spaces

- [ ] sound out words
  d-o-g = dog

- [ ] use a Period .

- [ ] Draw a picture

Name: ___________________  Date: ___________

Today is: Monday  Tuesday  Wednesday
          Thursday  Friday

Name: _________________________  Date: _______________

Today is:  Monday   Tuesday   Wednesday   Thursday   Friday

Direction: Read the words and make a sentence.

| jambon | confiture | mouton | palourde |
|---|---|---|---|
| ham | konfyt | skape | clam |

Name

Draw a Picture

## I Can...

- [ ] use a Capital Letter
  The cat is big.

- [ ] use spaces

- [ ] sound out words
  d-o-g = dog

- [ ] use a Period  .

- [ ] Draw a
  picture

Name: _______________________ Date: _______________

Today is: [Monday] [Tuesday] [Wednesday] [Thursday] [Friday]

Name: _______________________  Date: _______________

Today is: [Monday] [Tuesday] [Wednesday]
[Thursday] [Friday]

Direction: Read the words and make a sentence.

| lit | de premier plan | rouge | mariage |
|---|---|---|---|
| bed | voorste | rooi | troue |

Name

Draw a Picture

## I Can...

- [ ] use a Capital Letter
  The cat is big.

- [ ] use spaces

- [ ] sound out words
  d-o-g = dog

- [ ] use a Period .

- [ ] Draw a picture

Name: _______________________   Date: _______________

Today is: [ Monday ] [ Tuesday ] [ Wednesday ]
[ Thursday ] [ Friday ]

Direction: Read the words and make a sentence.

| mauvais | papa | furieux | triste |
|---|---|---|---|
| slegte | pa | mal | hartseer |

# Name

Draw a Picture

## I Can...

- ☐ use a Capital Letter
  The cat is big.

- ☐ use spaces

- ☐ sound out words
  d-o-g = dog

- ☐ use a Period  .

- ☐ Draw a picture

Name: ___________________    Date: ___________

Today is:   Monday    Tuesday    Wednesday

Thursday    Friday

Name: _________________________ Date: _____________

Today is: Monday Tuesday Wednesday
Thursday Friday

Direction: Read the words and make a sentence.

| animal den | poule | écuries | dix |
|---|---|---|---|
| den | hen | stalle | tien |

Name

Draw a Picture

## I Can...

- [ ] use a Capital Letter
  The cat is big.

- [ ] use spaces

- [ ] sound out words
  d-o-g = dog

- [ ] use a Period .

- [ ] Draw a picture

Name: _______________________ Date: _______________

Today is: Monday Tuesday Wednesday
Thursday Friday

Name: _______________________  Date: _______________

Today is: [ Monday ] [ Tuesday ] [ Wednesday ]
[ Thursday ] [ Friday ]

Direction: Read the words and make a sentence.

| gommeux | maman | somme | tambour |
|---|---|---|---|
| gummy | mamma | som | drom |

Name
_______________________________

Draw a Picture

## I Can...

- ☐ use a Capital Letter
  <u>T</u>he cat is big.

- ☐ use spaces

- ☐ sound out words
  d-o-g = dog

- ☐ use a Period .

- ☐ Draw a picture

Name: _______________________ Date: _______________

Today is: Monday Tuesday Wednesday Thursday Friday

Name: _______________________  Date: _______________

Today is: [ Monday ] [ Tuesday ] [ Wednesday ]
          [ Thursday ] [ Friday ]

Direction: Read the words and make a sentence.

| **offre** | **cacher** | **enfant** | **couvercle** |
|---|---|---|---|
| bod | verberg | kind | deksel |

Name

Draw a Picture

## I Can...

- [ ] use a Capital Letter
  The cat is big.

- [ ] use spaces

- [ ] sound out words
  d-o-g = dog

- [ ] use a Period .

- [ ] Draw a picture

Name: _______________________   Date: _______________

Today is:  Monday  Tuesday  Wednesday  Thursday  Friday

Name: _________________________ Date: _______________

Today is: Monday  Tuesday  Wednesday  Thursday  Friday

Direction: Read the words and make a sentence.

| gros | creuser | porc | perruque |
|------|---------|------|----------|
| groot | grawe | vark | wig |

Draw a Picture

I Can...

use a Capital Letter
The cat is big.

use spaces

sound out words
d-o-g = dog

use a Period .

Draw a
picture

Name: _______________________  Date: _______________

Today is:  [ Monday ]  [ Tuesday ]  [ Wednesday ]
           [ Thursday ]  [ Friday ]

Name: _________________________ Date: _______________

Today is: Monday  Tuesday  Wednesday

Thursday  Friday

Direction: Read the words and make a sentence.

| poubelle | ailette | épingle | gagner |
|---|---|---|---|
| bin | vin | speld | wen |

# Name

Draw a Picture

## I Can...

- [ ] use a Capital Letter
  The cat is big.

- [ ] use spaces

- [ ] sound out words
  d-o-g = dog

- [ ] use a Period .

- [ ] Draw a picture

Name: ___________________  Date: ___________

Today is: Monday  Tuesday  Wednesday
          Thursday  Friday

Name: _____________    Date: _____________

Today is: Monday  Tuesday  Wednesday
          Thursday  Friday

Direction: Read the words and make a sentence.

| hanche | lèvres | pincer | boisson |
|---|---|---|---|
| hip | lippe | nip | drink |

Name

Draw a Picture

## I Can...

- [ ] use a Capital Letter
  The cat is big.

- [ ] use spaces

- [ ] sound out words
  d-o-g = dog

- [ ] use a Period .

- [ ] Draw a picture

Name: _______________________  Date: _______________________

Today is:  Monday   Tuesday   Wednesday   Thursday   Friday

Name: _________________________  Date: _________________

Today is: [Monday] [Tuesday] [Wednesday]
[Thursday] [Friday]

Direction: Read the words and make a sentence.

| en forme | frappé | trousse | asseoir |
|----------|--------|---------|---------|
| fiks | getref | kit | sit |

Name

## Draw a Picture

## I Can...

- [ ] use a Capital Letter
  The cat is big.

- [ ] use spaces

- [ ] sound out words
  d-o-g = dog

- [ ] use a Period .

- [ ] Draw a picture

Name: _______________________  Date: _______________

Today is: Monday  Tuesday  Wednesday  Thursday  Friday

Name: ___________________  Date: ___________________

Today is: Monday  Tuesday  Wednesday

Thursday  Friday

Direction: Read the words and make a sentence.

| blé | emploi | rob | pleurer |
|---|---|---|---|
| koring | werk | beroof | geroep |

Name ___________________________

<table>
<tr><td>

Draw a Picture

</td><td>

## I Can...

☐ use a Capital Letter
The cat is big.

☐ use spaces

☐ sound out words
d-o-g = dog

☐ use a Period .

☐ Draw a picture

</td></tr>
</table>

Name: _______________________  Date: _______________

Today is: Monday  Tuesday  Wednesday  Thursday  Friday

Name: _______________  Date: _______________

Today is: Monday  Tuesday  Wednesday

Thursday  Friday

Direction: Read the words and make a sentence.

| chien | porc | le jogging | bois |
|---|---|---|---|
| hond | hog | draf | hout |

Name

Draw a Picture

## I Can...

- [ ] use a Capital Letter
  The cat is big.

- [ ] use spaces

- [ ] sound out words
  d-o-g = dog

- [ ] use a Period .

- [ ] Draw a
  picture

Name: ___________________  Date: ___________

Today is: [ Monday ] [ Tuesday ] [ Wednesday ]
[ Thursday ] [ Friday ]

Name: _______________________    Date: _______________

Today is: [ Monday ] [ Tuesday ] [ Wednesday ]
[ Thursday ] [ Friday ]

Direction: Read the words and make a sentence.

| punaise | étreinte | cruche | agresser |
| --- | --- | --- | --- |
| fout | drukkie | beker | beker |

Name

### Draw a Picture

## I Can...

- [ ] use a Capital Letter
  <u>T</u>he cat is big.

- [ ] use spaces

- [ ] sound out words
  d-o-g = dog

- [ ] use a Period .

- [ ] Draw a picture

Name: _______________    Date: _______________

Today is: Monday  Tuesday  Wednesday

Thursday  Friday

Name: _________________________  Date: _________________

Today is: [Monday] [Tuesday] [Wednesday]
[Thursday] [Friday]

Direction: Read the words and make a sentence.

| lit | point | chaud | pot |
|-----|-------|-------|-----|
| bed | dot | warm | pot |

Name

Draw a Picture

## I Can...

- [ ] use a Capital Letter
  The cat is big.

- [ ] use spaces

- [ ] sound out words
  d-o-g = dog

- [ ] use a Period .

- [ ] Draw a picture

Name: _______________________  Date: _______________

Today is:  Monday   Tuesday   Wednesday
           Thursday   Friday